VENDANGE TARDIVE

Work by Peter Reading

Collected Poems: 1: POEMS 1970-1984 (Bloodaxe Books, 1995)

Water and Waste (1970), *For the Municipality's Elderly* (1974),
The Prison Cell & Barrel Mystery (1976), *Nothing For Anyone* (1977),
Fiction (1979), *Tom o' Bedlam's Beauties* (1981), *Diplopic* (1983),
5x5x5x5x5 (1983), *C* (1984)

Collected Poems: 2: POEMS 1985-1996 (Bloodaxe Books, 1996)

Ukulele Music (1985), *Going On* (1985), *Stet* (1986),
Final Demands (1988), *Perduta Gente* (1989), *Shitheads* (1989),
Evagatory (1992), *Last Poems* (1994), *Eschatological* (1996)

Collected Poems: 3: POEMS 1997-2003 (Bloodaxe Books, 2003)

Work in Regress (1997), *Ob.* (1999), *Marfan* (2000),
[untitled] (2001), *Faunal* (2002), *Civil* (2002)
♩ (2003)

-273.15 (Bloodaxe Books, 2005)
Vendange Tardive (Bloodaxe Books, 2010)

RECORDINGS

The Poetry Quartets: 3 (Bloodaxe Books/British Council, 1998)
   [with James Fenton, Tony Harrison & Ken Smith: 30 mins each]
The Life Works of Peter Reading (Lannan Foundation, 2003)
   [22 DVD videos: total length 22 hours: *see* www.lannan.org]

ON READING

Isabel Martin: *Reading Peter Reading* (Bloodaxe Books, 2000)

PETER READING
Vendange Tardive

BLOODAXE BOOKS

ISBN: 978 1 85224 884 0

First published 2010 by
Bloodaxe Books Ltd,
Highgreen,
Tarset,
Northumberland NE48 1RP.

www.bloodaxebooks.com
For further information about Bloodaxe titles
please visit our website or write to
the above address for a catalogue.

Supported by
**ARTS COUNCIL
ENGLAND**

Cover design: Neil Astley & Pamela Robertson-Pearce.

Printed in Great Britain by
Bell & Bain Limited, Glasgow, Scotland.

For the attention of Penelope Reading
(Nunc scio quid sit Amor)

ACKNOWLEDGEMENTS

Some of the material in this book was first published in *The Times Literary Supplement* and *The Wolf*, and on www.qualm.co.uk. 'Maritime' was commissioned by BBC Radio 3 and was subsequently published by Cleveland State University Program in Linguistics.

CONTENTS

DÖNNHOFF

Oberhäuser Brücke
Riesling Eiswein

1998

ERZEUGERABFÜLLUNG
WEINGUT HERMANN DÖNNHOFF D-55585 OBERHAUSEN/NAHE
QUALITÄTSWEIN MIT PRÄDIKAT A. P. Nr 775301002299
PRODUCE OF GERMANY

alc. 8.0% vol.   NAHE   375 ml e

'The harvest is passed, the summer is ended, and we are not saved.'

JEREMIAH VIII. 20

[Untitled]

The rhetorical 'How goes it, old boy?';
the unnerving response:

'Infinitely sad, old warrior,
infinitely sad – I've just heard...'.

Funerary

Parents soon die, it is their nature;
progeny shortly after, or before.

Father, brother, mother...

That which ought to be done
is presumed to have been done.

[When there is nothing,
eschew utterance.]

Vendange Tardive

a.m.,
27.vii.08 [62, eh?],
Gauguin on the card –
Harvest: Le Pouldu, 1890.

Fresh figs.
Puligny-Montrachet 1er Cru (Le Cailleret, 2001),
greenish gold meniscus,
faint smoke/melon palate...

Countering the day's tabloid shite,
gratitude to Gauguin,
Vincent Girardin
and Dr Greppin (donor of the splendid 750 ml.).

Maritime

In the year of 1609,
in a ship of 300 ton
with 160 persons
outward-bound for Virginia,
we was surprised with a most
extreme violent storm,
when our fine vessel, though new,
fell into a great leak
so as all hands and passengers
was forced for three days space
to exert ourselves to save us
from sinking unto the deep.
But notwithstanding incessant
pumping and casting out water
by buckets and all other means,
yet the brine swamped all the goods
within the hold, and all men
was exhausted and spent of strength,
gone to sleep, overcome with labour
and hopeless of any succour,
yielding ourselves to the mercy
of the sea's tempestuous onslaught.

After Poseidon had summoned the sea to
   mountainous fury,
wily Laertides quailed at the sight of a
   huge rolling breaker
heaving above his small craft, and the arch of it
   pounded down, powerful,
snatching the steering-oar out of his grip and
   snapping the stout mast,
flinging the yard and the sail to the furious
   hurricane, tossing
into the boiling brine the nimble-
   witted wanderer.
Weighted by clothes which the goddess Calypso had
   given him, he sunk,
having to battle to rise through the force of the
   mighty wave's downrush,
splutt'ring at last to the air and voiding
   brine from his nostrils.
Powerfully swimming, he regained his craft which was
   storm-pitched and broken,
stripped off his sodden garb, when malicious
   wrathful Poseidon
roused up another rogue wave to batter the
   vessel to matchwood.

Hilbre, winter, high tide.
Over the West Hoyle, hurl and white swash, and above,
the sky the colour of Blaenau Ffestiniog slate.
And the long-ruined sandstone lifeboat station brine-lashed,
the slipway thrashing the saline assault into spume.

Past the pyramidal buoy,
close to the wavetops and hurtling into the wind,
Red-throated Divers and Common Scoters and auks,
and the day was ornithologically unforgettable,
and the friend I was with then is fullfathomfive (as you might say).

Sir George Somers, at the stern,
observing the plight of the vessel,
desperate of relief,
looking every minute
when that the ship would sink,
he espied land which to his eyes,
and in Captain Newport's opinion,
was judged to be that dreadful
coast of the Bermodes,
which islands was full of all nations
and accounted to be enchanted
and inhabited by witches
and devils, which grew by reason
of monstrous thunder, storm,
and tempest near unto those isles,
also for that the whole
coast is so wondrous dangerous
of rocks that few can approach
but with unspeakable hazard
of surf thrashed high as whale-spouts
and incontrovertible shipwrack.

Hilbre under thick snow,
compacted ridges of two weeks' ice on the foreshore,
above the foam at the foot of the lifeboat slipway,
into the face of a Beaufort force seven, a flake-white
Larus hyperboreus (2nd winter);

and over the flat of the Hoyle,
creaming and distantly sibilant flow-tide breakers
flushed up a fast-wheeling blizzard of silver and white
Calidris alba, and Donahue (thirty years dead)
observed that he wouldn't forget this day till he died.

As severe seas pounded our hull,
Sir Thomas Gates, Captain Newport
and Sir George Somers agreed
of two evils, to choose the least.
So, in desperate resolution,
they directed our vessel towards
those islands, where our ship,
by God's Divine Providence,
ran fast, at the rise of a roller,
between two vasty rocks,
where it lodged, wedged, without splint'ring.
And we hoisted out our boat,
and we landed all of those persons
in good safety, and, come on shore,
we was soon refreshed and cheered.
Though salt water did great spoil
to most of our lading and victuals,
yet some meal was well recovered,
and many particular things
for our common use was preserved;
and the soil and the air seemed sweet.

Two days and nights he was lost in the swollen
    waves, but the third dawn,
winds ceased and breathless calm came; a gently
    rising roller
revealed to the shipwrecked yet ever resourceful
    son of Laertes
sweet land wooded with cypress and cedar not
    half-a-league distant.
When he had swum close into the coast, though,
    all hope quit him –
angrily-roaring great seas were battering
    jagged rock outcrops,
misting the shore with fine-pounded spume-clouds in
    precipitation,
no cove or haven, but headlands of rugged
    knife-sharp cliff-face.
Then he was suddenly borne by a riptide
    into the crashing
barnacle-crusted crags and buttresses.
    In desperation,
boldly the wily-witted Laertides
    grasped a rough outcrop.
Then, as the swell receded, its backwash
    once more swamped him,
flinging him far out to sea, there were flesh shreds
    flanched on the raw rock.
Thus does impartial Poseidon apportion us
    infinite big shit.

Family Album

The father:
oxygen, tubes, analgesic.
The brother:
tubes, analgesic, oxygen.
The mother:
analgesic, oxygen, tubes...

[The bereaved:
precognition, occurrence.]

I.M. **G.E.** (1916-95)

I don't normally
chat with those who've popped their clogs.
Nevertheless… What
do you think of this? – it's called
'The Gavin Ewart
5/8/5 Haiku':

When they first heard my
Sonata for two Steamrollers
they were enruptured.

Putney, from the Duke's,
a lone craft is launched
into the sable current,
1995.

Inflationary

In the old days
you would have been charged
one *obolos* to cross.

There became so many passengers
that the Authorities
had to lay on more ferries.

Today it will cost you
1,200 euros, £1,000, 1,377 U.S. bucks, 130,380 yen
to achieve the further bank.

[Fragmentary]

When there is nothing, —
eschew utterance. —

All is safely gathered in

Morituri te salutant,
Alan Jenkins, whom we can't repay
since you fêted us with Clicquot
on our bacchanalian nuptial day.

Harvest, and the neutral combine
shears the puny full-grown to the stubble
(*fetch the shoebox, fetch the shovel,* as a chap might say).
Toodle-pip (and don't think *you'll* be very far away).

Dönnhoff Oberhäuser Brücke
Riesling Eiswein 1998, 375 ml.,

colour, old gold
as Grandmother's wedding ring
assayed in 1900
24 carat.

Nose, intense, honeyed,
mineral/acid-balanced.

Palate, confirming all these
together with profound fruit.

Picked late from the frozen vine,
this Qualitätswein mit Prädikat,
lusciously concentrating
fructose, has even countered
the tabloids' and broadsheets' faecal
facts slapped daily
onto the cheap lino.

Exponential

Haven't been reading our Malthus *have* we?

(Population, unchecked,
increases exponentially, whereas
subsistence merely stays about the same.)

Beget brat – Council flat.

Fabulous

Demeter tutored Triptolemus
in agriculture and lent him
her winged chariot, wherein
he traversed the globe, regaled
the Third World with grain...

[Oh *yeah*.]

...and another thing, Johnston,

Provincetown, outwardbound
to observe a couple of Humpbacks.

As the flukes sunk easefully, splashless,
a fluster of Wilson's Storm Petrel,
and funereal Sooty Shearwater
(fast shallow beats, short glides).

Let's certainly observe
we've had a good time of it, you
and Penelope and I...

Breakwater's bleak heap,
Black-crowned Night Heron, hunched,
anticipating our moorage.

Exponential

Population, energy, food,
    headline MORE AUTOMOBILES
    TO GET US BACK ON OUR FEET...

Meanwhile CIPEC and OPEC won't
give it away, we must Shell out –
    or, atavistically, war.

Nycticorax nycticorax

That Black-crowned Night Heron,
is it Osirian?

Mneh!, just some dumb bird.

And Now, a Quick Look at the Morning Papers

creasing numbe
  eenage pregnanc
fficial figures reinforce
  ngland's position the Europ
eenage capital of pregnanc About
  40 in every 1,000 schoolgirls in Engl
is growing concern about Britain's
  youth sex culture following cl
12-year-old boy fathered a
  15-year-old girl given b
twins fathered by a cla
  her mother, Janet 'I
he stayed here the
  odd night and of
course it happe

church
  denounces
moves in Spai
  to legalis
abortio

no respite in the killing fields
  markets around world in turm
suddenly everyone is leavin
  Las Vegas

Exponential

These are the days of the phoney. Hanging
   on by the fingernails,
frantic contortions, impotent, aimed at
perpetuation of obsolescent
   oil-based economies.

27.VII.09

[63, eh? Hmmm…
Vendange Tardive, and all that.
    Nearly combine time.]

Clockwise (from the bottom),

4 degrees Celsius up,
40 years on: Antarctic
glacial meltdown, ergo,
sea levels risen (albeit
most marine life extinct).

South America: deluge,
deglaciation, desert,
uninhabitable
(by humankind, that is).

North America: drought,
flood, hurricane, desert,
uninhabitable
(by humankind, that is).

Canada: now warm, fertile
(all hands battle to live there).

Greenland's icesheet thawed.

#

Scandinavia/UK/
Russia/Siberia:
ideal growing conditions
(all hands war to get there).

Southern Europe: desert,
snow-free Alps, dry rivers.

Middle East: same old testament.

Asia: Himalayan
deglaciation, floods;
Bangladesh abandoned,
ditto South India,
Pakistan &c.

Southern China: dried rivers
and aquifers mean
the region is abandoned,
monsoons erode the earth,
dustbowls only obtain.

Polynesia: sunk.

Australia: in the north,
and in Tas., 'compact cities' –
all hands at war to get there –
the mass is wilderness.

New Zealand: densely populous,
intensive farming and all that
(all hands, &c., &c...

Exponential

The corn-coloured neutral combine –
  first we see is its shadow
  approaching, swathing hectares.

All things in season: steady thresh,
the dark swift coming and going,
  Dow-Jones average, fin., fin.

[Untitled]

Recent research suggests
the improbability of thunder
being caused by god's bollocks jangling
(*tantum religio potuit*
suadere malorium).

In the land of Moab
there lies a lonely grave.
Many are eyeless
in the Gaza Strip.

Yen, Euro, Sterling,
Buck, Dinar, fin.

Many could be worse off;
many couldn't (Sudan,
Zimbabwe...).

Amazon rainforest fucked,
S & N Poles ditto.

This black marble bust
of Amenhoptep III, who ruled
3,400 years ago,
has just been dug up.

This spectacular image

of the Helix nebula
was taken with the Wide
Field Imager telescope
at the La Silla Observatory
in Chile. The Helix,
dying suns burning out,
spinning out rings of gas
and dust two light years across,
lies about 700
light years from this planet.

Tri

well-fancied Bensalem
has been ruled out
of tomorrow's Albert Bartlett
Novices' Hurdle at Cheltenham
after a dirty scope

Diane reprimands Val
for hiding her plans for the Woolpack
and Mark is furious to learn
the pub is not on the market

Andy and Daz
have a brawl with Aaron
(S) 9218

vintage Ryan
is cut above
to put inter outta

very real peril
UK will go bankrupt

4,000 cheer our boys

Abdullah wants UK
to be ruled by Sharia law

the world's oldest shoe
preserved for 5,000 years
has been found at Lake Constance, Germany

In the Beginning, *H. sap.*
was scared to shit by Zeus
et al., enter our hero,
Epicurus, yelling 'Twaddle!,
this here's Physics, not mumbo-
jumbo – gerroutofit!
How much idiot evil
gormless theists engender.'

this asteroid entered the atmosphere
in about one second, warming
the air in front of it
to many times the temperature
of the sun.

On impact it vaporised,

melted blobs of bedrock

matter ejected fell back to earth at high speeds

like trillions of meteors
heated on reentry
ignited forest fires

end of Mesozoic

endof

A Shropshire Lad

I was working along with Davies,
it was probably '76,
anyhow, it was a drought year,
midsummer and no grazing,
we were grafting through the nightshift
at Farmore (South Shropshire Farmers)
in the Arms. We were operating
the Pacepacker, bagging off
Cattle High Protein Pellets
when the machine busted on us.

Tony did his crust
and kicked the stitching machine
to shit with his steel-toecapped boots.

Just now, into the warehouse,
enters the Boss, white-coated.
'Something awry, Tony?'

'Well, look at the fuckin fucker,
the fuckin fucker's fuckin fucked.'
(He was a great lad, Tony,
for his use of the metaphor.)

The Gaffer has gone, long, long.

As for Tony Davies,
he is (sort of) immortal.
A great lad for the metaphor –
'Look at the fuckin fucker,
the fuckin fucker's fuckin fucked.'

A great lad for the metaphor.

What the Papers Say

Meet shameless Kevin
and Elizabeth Crawford
who falsely claimed
£50,000 in disabled benefits despite being healthy

More people know
how to set up a Facebook page
how to set up
than to change a plug
                     plug

MOSHA the first elephant
to be fitted with
a prosthetic leg
after she stepped on a landmine
two years ago

sex tape gigolo who blackmailed
BMW heiress is jailed for six

people who believe the weather
can bring on a headache are right,
scientists have found

Rosslyn Morgan, 80,
has played cornet in a brass
band at Ystradgnlais,
Powys, since 1936 –
and never missed a practice

Three times

SYMBOLIC ACT OF
RENEWED TERROR

Fail

ATTACKING the British Army
...this is potent act of symbolism
...that a new IRA
...proving to themselves it is in the

ending to
s lying still
was blood
place was
tell who
re.
attack.
in a

helpline NHS Direct and a nurse
told her to demand a home visit
from a doctor as soon as possible.
At 12.20pm she called Pri...
But was it an refusa...

when the IRA
Book Parcles Stephen
Restored at 22

...tacted the family GP. But
...cause it was a Saturday she was
...an out of hours service
...pital Ger...

BOMB 'CONFESSION'

questions supp...
...ut my situation wor...
...d me cat

use in.
the rea
Geov.
favour a
quick as i
Feted fc
winning go.
season Manc
the midfield.
surplus to rep.
He recall.
Manchester City.
i't matches and
three goals but l
have any more real c
in the team.
"I still don't know why
Eriksson didn't trust me. If
he'd trusted me, like Phil
does, maybe I'd
have per
formed better

was a dedicated soldier
ready to risk his life
for the Afghan people. IRA
executioners
ensured he never

better at claiming benefits
than darning a pair of socks

open a Facebook account:
70% can do it

rewire a plug: 68%

schools react to father aged 13
with sex lessons for five-year-olds

bake your own bread
to stop feeling bloated

can peaches and pears make me fat?

SVG slump

Share prices updated
every two minutes
throughout the day
at WWW.THISISMONEY.CO.UK

tax scam

Envoi

How common are Earthlike planets?

Start with the number of galaxies:
estimate that it's more than
100,000,000,000.

How many stars in a galaxy? –
circa 100 billion?
That puts the number of stars
at 100 billion multiplied
by 100 billion.

NASA suggests that approx.
7% of nearly
all stars host a giant planet,
and that the number of planets
around each star increases
as the planet's mass decreases
toward the size of Earth.

From these lucubrations,
call it 1 billion trillion
Earthlike planets in this
(what's thought as) universe

From the Creative Writing Stint

"Sweet-zephyr-movèd-nimbus, who can tell
which drifty course you may pursue anon?"

[V ash, test fallout, aviation fuel . . .]

"Poor flackering, oilèd seafowl – who can know
what suff'ring you may have to undergo?"

[BP, BP, BP, BP, BP . . .]

PETER READING

TLS JULY 16 2010